XTREME
RESCUES

TRAPPED
IN A THAILAND CAVE

S.L. HAMILTON

A&D Xtreme
An imprint of Abdo Publishing
abdobooks.com

abdobooks.com

Published by Abdo Publishing, a division of ABDO, PO Box 398166, Minneapolis, Minnesota 55439.
Copyright © 2020 by Abdo Consulting Group, Inc. International copyrights reserved in all countries.
No part of this book may be reproduced in any form without written permission from the publisher.
A&D Xtreme™ is a trademark and logo of Abdo Publishing.

Printed in the United States of America, North Mankato, MN.
092019
012020

Editor: John Hamilton
Copy Editor: Bridget O'Brien
Graphic Design: Sue Hamilton & Dorothy Toth
Cover Design: Victoria Bates
Cover Photo: AP
Interior Photos & Illustrations:
Alamy-pgs 18-19, 22-23 & 30-31;
AP-pgs 1, 4-5, 6-7, 8-9, 12-13, 16-17 (inset)
24-25 & 26-27 (top & bottom);
Getty-pgs 2-3,10-11, 14-15 & 32;
Javier Zarracina/Vox-pg 22 (inset);
Royal Thai Navy SEALs-pg 20 (inset) & pgs 20-21;
Shutterstock-pgs 28-29; SWNS-pg 16-17.

Library of Congress Control Number: 2019941919
Publisher's Cataloging-in-Publication Data

Names: Hamilton, S.L., author.
Title: Trapped in a Thailand cave / by S.L. Hamilton
Description: Minneapolis, Minnesota : Abdo Publishing, 2020 | Series: Xtreme rescues | Includes online
    resources and index.
Identifiers: ISBN 9781532190063 (lib. bdg.) | ISBN 9781644943540 (pbk.) | ISBN 9781532175916 (ebook)
Subjects: LCSH: Caves--Thailand--Juvenile literature. | Tham Phā Lāi (Thailand)--Juvenile literature. |
    Soccer teams--Juvenile literature. | Caving--Search and rescue operations--Juvenile literature. |
    Monsoons--Juvenile literature.
Classification: DDC 363.348--dc23

CONTENTS

THAILAND CAVE RESCUE

Twelve boys and their soccer coach entered Thailand's Tham Luang cave on the afternoon of June 23, 2018. Monsoon rains caused the cave to quickly fill with water. They were trapped.

In the days ahead, search and rescue efforts took place involving people from around the world. Government officials, divers, police officers, soldiers, medical personnel, and aid workers came together to locate the boys and their coach, and to rescue them from the cave.

Rescuers gather at the mouth of Tham Luang cave, while the trapped boys' bikes sit waiting for them to return.

RAIN AND DANGER

Tham Luang's name means "cave of the sleeping lady."
The limestone cave is 6.4 miles (10.3 km) long. It has a large
main entrance, but narrows into thin, winding tunnels.
Water always flows through the cave.

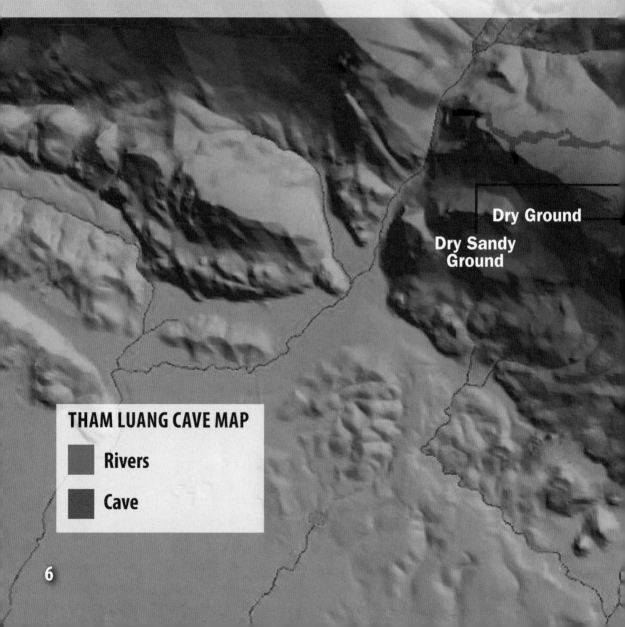

Dry Ground

Dry Sandy
Ground

THAM LUANG CAVE MAP

Rivers

Cave

The cave is open to the public from November to June. It is closed July to October. This is when heavy monsoon rains come to the area. A "danger" sign sits at the entrance to the cave, warning visitors about the flooding during the rainy season.

Rainy Season
Flood Water
Enters The Cave
From This Direction

Bikes Parked

Entrance

MISSING

By the evening of June 23, 2018, the boys had not come home. Worried parents contacted head coach Nopparat Khanthawong. He found out that assistant coach Ekkaphon Chanthawong (Coach Ek) and twelve members of the Wild Boars junior soccer team had gone to explore Tham Luang cave.

Rushing to the cave, Coach Khanthawong discovered the boys' bikes and soccer equipment at the entrance. Khanthawong was afraid that his assistant coach and the boys were trapped inside. He contacted officials and parents. Several people tried to get into the cave, but the water was too high. No one knew how they would find the 13 missing people or even if they were still alive.

THE WORLD FINDS OUT

On June 24, 2018, experienced cavers discovered that water had risen to Tham Luang's ceiling in many areas. Cave scuba diving experts were needed to find the missing 13.

Thai Navy SEALs were called in. They dove in the muddy water and narrow, winding passages to place air supplies and safety guidelines. But they were not experienced cave divers. More help was needed. By June 26, international search and rescue experts arrived at Tham Luang. News crews reported all the latest efforts. The rescue story had reached the world.

ABOVEGROUND RESCUE EFFORTS

Rescuers needed to get into the cave. No one knew if the missing 13 were alive or dead. Pumps were set up to siphon off the water and empty it through hoses. But the monsoon rains quickly refilled the cave.

Pipes and hoses channel water out of Tham Luang cave.

Engineers knew they needed to stop water from entering the cave through sinkholes and other aboveground openings. They built a network of plastic and bamboo pipes that channeled the rain down the mountain. After a day, water levels finally began to go down. They could walk in parts of the cave.

XTREME QUOTE

"It's like turning the faucet on and trying to siphon water off at the same time. There's only so much you can do."
—Joshua Morris, Caving & Expedition Leader

CAVE DIVERS ARRIVE

On June 27, four days since the 13 were trapped in the cave, members of the British Cave Rescue Council (BCRC) made their first dive inside Tham Luang. The experienced rescuers found the cave had the worst possible diving conditions.

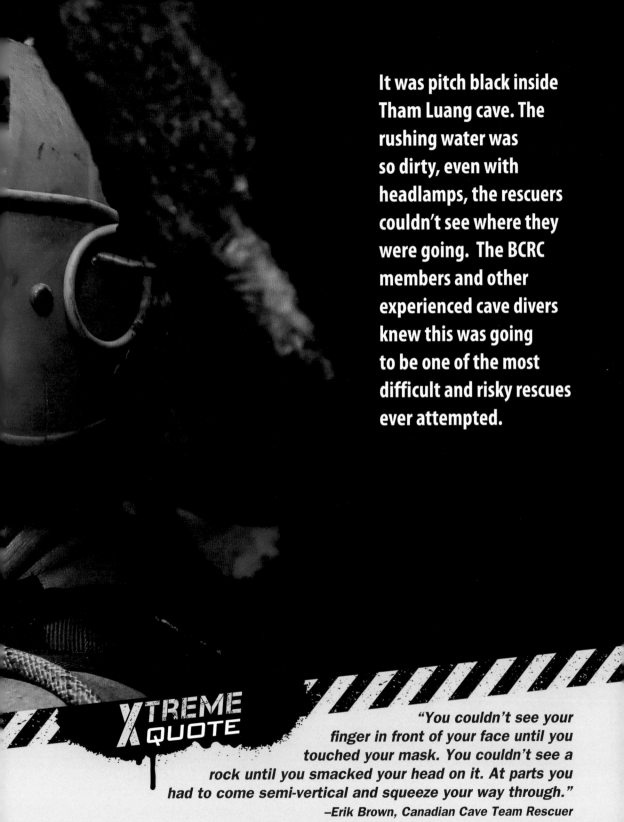

It was pitch black inside Tham Luang cave. The rushing water was so dirty, even with headlamps, the rescuers couldn't see where they were going. The BCRC members and other experienced cave divers knew this was going to be one of the most difficult and risky rescues ever attempted.

FOUND ALIVE!

On July 2, 2018, BCRC divers Rick Stanton and John Volanthen were able to dive farther into the cave. They swam in near zero visibility. They reached a high area named Pattaya Beach, but the 13 weren't there. Stanton and Volanthen had enough air to dive a little longer. They surfaced in the next air pocket and found Coach Ek and all 12 boys alive and well, but very hungry! While the world cheered the news, the problem of getting them out was just beginning.

One of the first images of the 12 boys and their coach.

BCRC divers Rick Stanton (left) and John Volanthen found the missing 13.

XTREME FACT

Coach Ek and the boys tried to dig their way out of the cave using pieces of rock. They had chipped a hole 16.4 feet (5 m) long by the time they were found.

RESCUE OPTIONS

Rescuers had three options:

1) Wait for the water to go down. The 13 could stay for several months until the monsoon season was over and the water drained naturally. But oxygen was being used up faster than it could seep into the cave. They would run out of air.

2) Drill a shaft.
Drilling through the mountain would take at least a month, and if the pumps stopped working, water would fill the cave and they would drown.

3) Swim out using diving gear. This was the quickest and most dangerous option. None of the 13 knew how to scuba dive. It was risky, but also the best choice to save their lives.

Rescuers discuss options to save the missing 13.

TRAGEDY

How dangerous this mission was became clear on July 6, 2018. Volunteer diver Saman Guana placed air tanks along the cave route, preparing the way to get the boys out. The 37 year old was a former Thai Navy SEAL and a skilled diver. But while swimming through the cold water, Saman ran out of oxygen. He died in the cave. If an experienced cave diver could die, could the 13 make it out alive?

Saman Guana

Tham Luang cave divers risked their own lives to rescue the 13.

Get Them Out Now!

Thailand's weather forecast was for very heavy rains. This threat made officials decide to get the 13 out right away using diving gear. However, there was still the problem that the inexperienced boys and coach might be terrified in the murky water and tight areas of the cave. Panic could lead to death. To keep everyone safe, the 13 would use a full face mask and have medicine to relax them. They would be carried out in a Sked stretcher by rescuers.

First Diver

Second Diver

Full Face Mask
on Boy

Boy's
Oxygen Tank

Guide Rope

Sked Stretcher

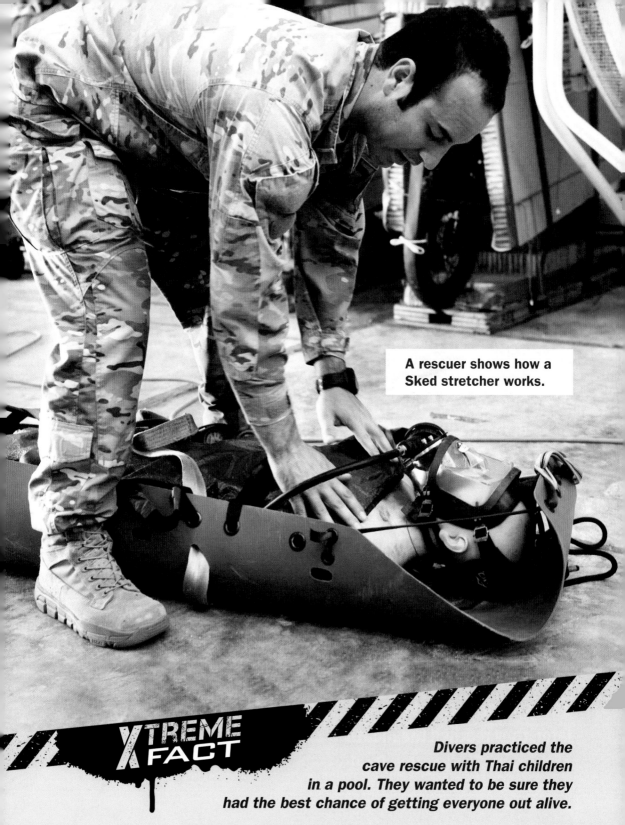

A rescuer shows how a Sked stretcher works.

X TREME FACT

Divers practiced the cave rescue with Thai children in a pool. They wanted to be sure they had the best chance of getting everyone out alive.

The Rescue Begins

On July 8, 2018, the rescue began. Five Thai Navy SEALs and 13 foreign divers swam 3 hours to the trapped soccer team. The boys, coach, and Thai divers chose the rescue order and the first boy's journey out began. He was tethered to one BCRC diver, and together they dove under the water. Other rescuers waited throughout the cave. They checked the boy's face mask and changed the air tanks. He was moved across muddy but unflooded areas. Sometimes this even involved pulling the boy in his stretcher across high-rope lines that had been strung across rough areas. Hours later, they reached the mouth of the cave. The boy was free!

All 13 Rescued

One by one, the trapped team members made the trip out of Tham Luang cave. Four boys were rescued on days 1 and 2. Five came out on day 3. By July 10, 2018, all the boys and their coach were successfully rescued. It had been 18 days since they were trapped. The rescue happened just in time. Many of the water pumps had stopped working. Water was rising in the cave again. The rescuers had to get out quickly. It was dangerous, but everyone escaped before floodwaters filled the cave.

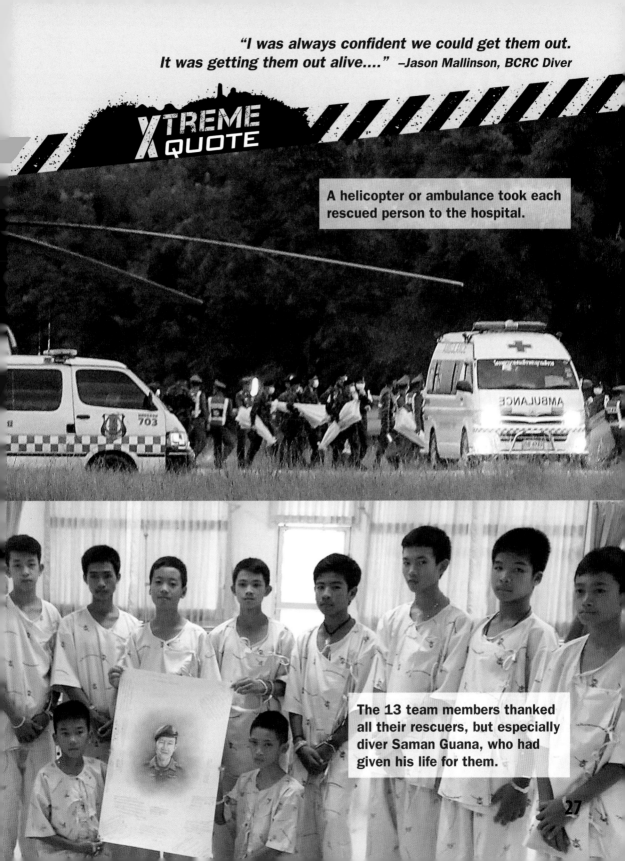

"I was always confident we could get them out. It was getting them out alive...." –Jason Mallinson, BCRC Diver

A helicopter or ambulance took each rescued person to the hospital.

The 13 team members thanked all their rescuers, but especially diver Saman Guana, who had given his life for them.

27

WHAT IF IT HAPPENS TO YOU?

The most important factor to survive being trapped in a cave is to stay calm. Do not panic. Be sure to let other people know you are entering a cave. If you get trapped, follow these steps:

1) Go caving with one or more people and stay together.

2) Find a safe location and stay there.

3) Use your flashlight or headlamp only when needed.

4) Carry emergency food and water. If you don't have either, remember that an average, inactive person can survive with only water for up to a month. In general, it is safer to sip the water that drips from the cave's ceilings and walls, rather than what may flow across the cave floor.

5) Listen for sounds of rescuers and be ready to yell or bang on the cave walls to signal them.

Coach Ek taught meditation to the boys to help them control their fear.

XTREME FACT

Glossary

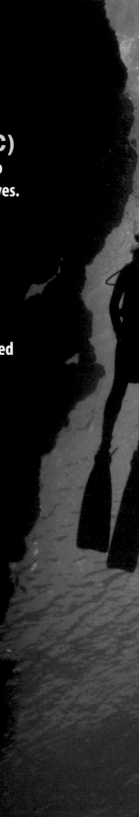

British Cave Rescue Council (BCRC)
Experienced cave divers from the United Kingdom who volunteer to help rescue people trapped in flooded caves.

Channel
A way to direct the course of water, such as through a pipe, hose, or long, narrow ditch.

Headlamp
A bright, lightweight, long-lasting light source mounted on a helmet or head strap that allows hands-free use. Usually worn by cave explorers, many types are also waterproof. Also called a headlight.

Limestone
A hard rock formed from the fossilized remains of shells or coral.

Meditation
A calming, mindful practice using the brain to control one's thoughts. A person often focuses on their breathing or repeats a certain word or sound called a mantra.

Monsoon
Heavy rains that fall in an area during certain months of the year. These seasonal rains often result in flooding.

SCUBA
Equipment that allows divers to breathe underwater without a hose attached to the surface or other air supply. Scuba stands for "self contained underwater breathing apparatus."

SIPHON
To empty a liquid (such as water) through a tube from one place to another lower area using pumps and/or atmospheric pressure to force the liquid out.

SKED STRETCHER
A stretcher designed for protecting and safely moving a person either horizontally or vertically, especially in caves or other tight places. Also called a drag stretcher.

THAI
A short form of Thailand.

THAI NAVY SEALS
Special operations soldiers of Thailand's Navy. They take their name from the elements in which they operate: sea, air, and land. SEALs are very well trained and perform some of the most dangerous missions.

ONLINE RESOURCES

Booklinks
NONFICTION NETWORK
FREE! ONLINE NONFICTION RESOURCES

To learn more about the Thailand cave rescue, visit abdobooklinks.com or scan this QR code. These links are routinely monitored and updated to provide the most current information available.

INDEX

A Thailand mural shows some of the 2018 Tham Luang cave rescuers.